# HOW ARE BABIES MADE?

Alastair Smith

Illustrated by Maria Wheatley

Designed by Ruth Russell

Digital artwork by Fiona Johnson

Series editor: Judy Tatchell

# There's a baby in there

All babies start inside their mothers. They grow and grow until they're big enough to live in the world outside.

## New babies

Even newborn babies look different from each other.

Some have lots of hair...

Some are big...

...Some have none at all.

...Some are small.

But all babies are made in the same way. This book will tell you how.

## Where does the baby grow?

The baby grows in a part of the body called the womb. Only girls and women have a womb.

The girl is pointing to where the womb is.

## Safe and sound

The baby has everything it needs inside its mother's womb. It is safe and warm. It grows there until it is ready to come out into the world.

## How long does the baby stay inside the mother?

A baby stays inside its mother for about nine months. So if it starts growing inside in January, it will be ready to come out in September.

| January | February | March | April | May | June |
|---------|----------|-------|-------|-----|------|
| ✔ | ✔ | ✔ | ✔ | ✔ | ✔ |
| July | August | September | October | November | December |
| ✔ | ✔ | ✱ | | | |

Now the baby has been growing inside for nine months.

## Why is it inside for so long?

That's how long it takes for a baby to grow. If it didn't grow enough, the baby might find it hard to stay alive in the world outside.

There's a baby growing inside this woman.

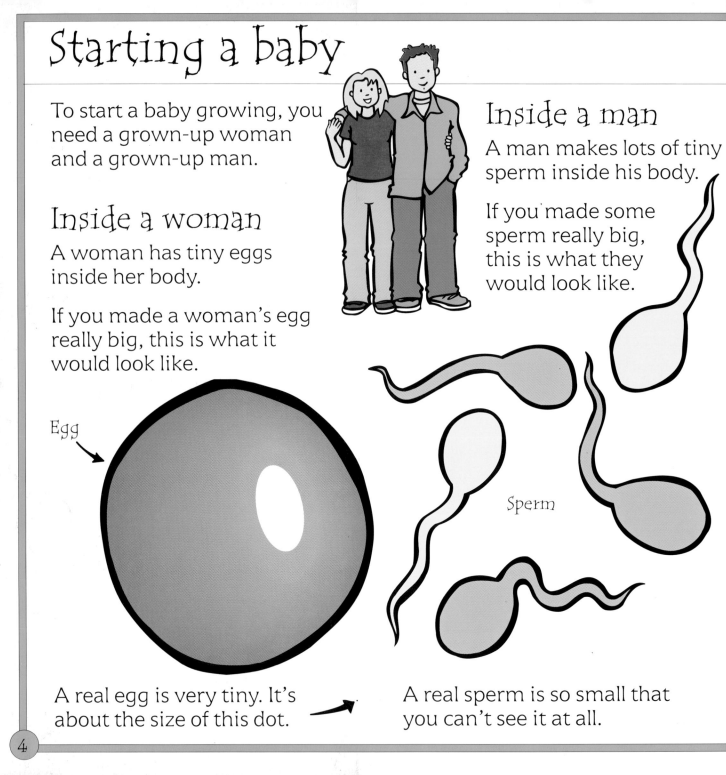

# Starting a baby

To start a baby growing, you need a grown-up woman and a grown-up man.

## Inside a woman

A woman has tiny eggs inside her body.

If you made a woman's egg really big, this is what it would look like.

Egg

A real egg is very tiny. It's about the size of this dot.

## Inside a man

A man makes lots of tiny sperm inside his body.

If you made some sperm really big, this is what they would look like.

Sperm

A real sperm is so small that you can't see it at all.

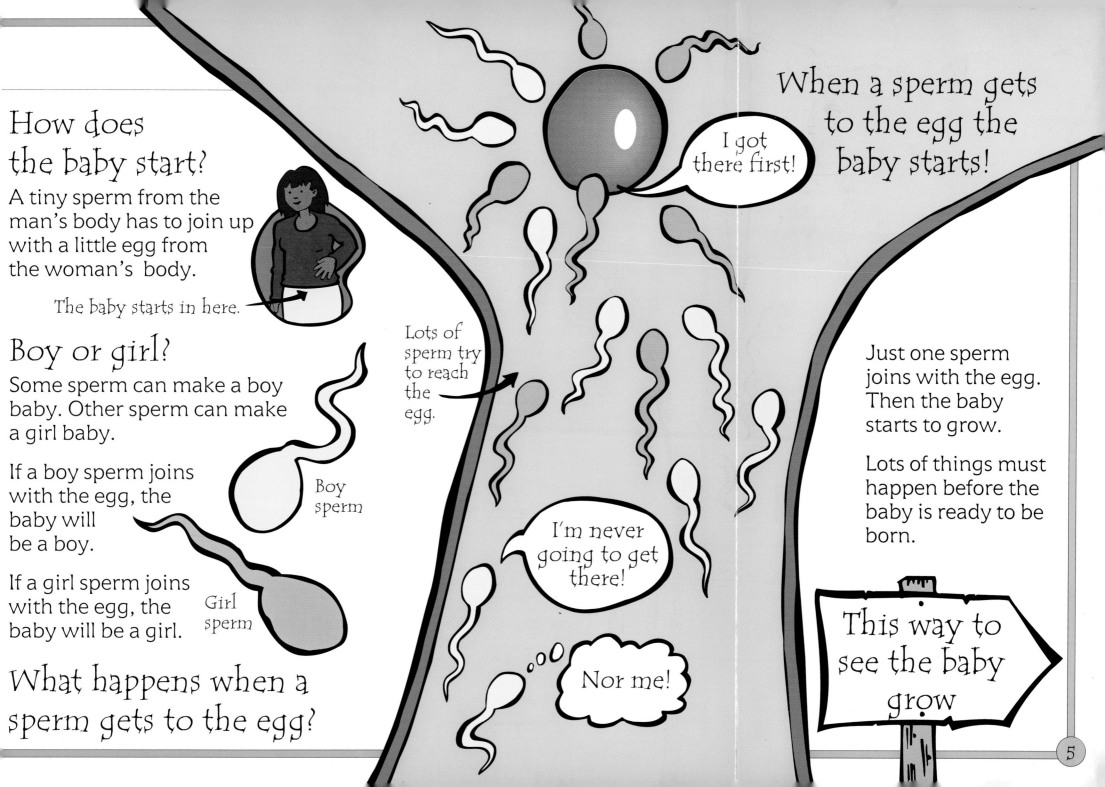

# How does the baby start?

A tiny sperm from the man's body has to join up with a little egg from the woman's body.

The baby starts in here.

# Boy or girl?

Some sperm can make a boy baby. Other sperm can make a girl baby.

If a boy sperm joins with the egg, the baby will be a boy.

Boy sperm

If a girl sperm joins with the egg, the baby will be a girl.

Girl sperm

# What happens when a sperm gets to the egg?

I got there first!

# When a sperm gets to the egg the baby starts!

Lots of sperm try to reach the egg.

Just one sperm joins with the egg. Then the baby starts to grow.

Lots of things must happen before the baby is ready to be born.

I'm never going to get there!

Nor me!

This way to see the baby grow

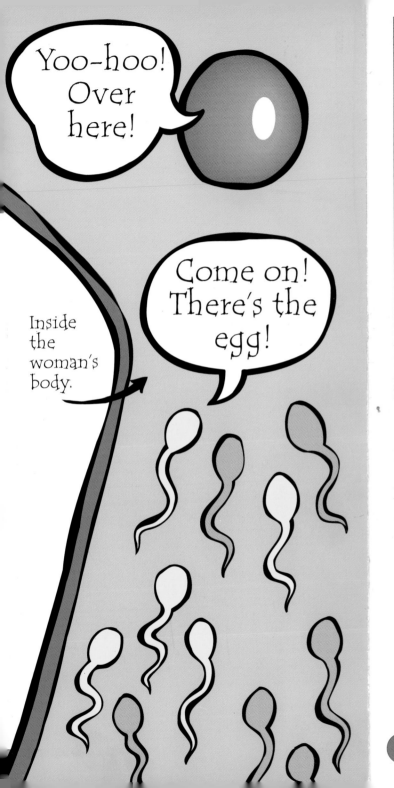

Yoo-hoo! Over here!

Come on! There's the egg!

Inside the woman's body.

## Life inside

The baby changes and grows a lot while it is inside its mother's womb.

### Does the baby show?

To begin with, the baby doesn't show at all. But on the inside, the woman's body is changing. It is getting ready to grow the baby.

The changes can make her feel tired.

sickly feeling

She might feel a little sick.

She needs to eat lots of good food.

# Food and drink

Soon after the baby starts, a tube grows between it and its mother.

The tube carries all the food and drink that the baby needs. It goes into the baby's body.

The mother's body shares all the things that she eats and drinks with her baby.

Your belly button is the place where your tube went into you.

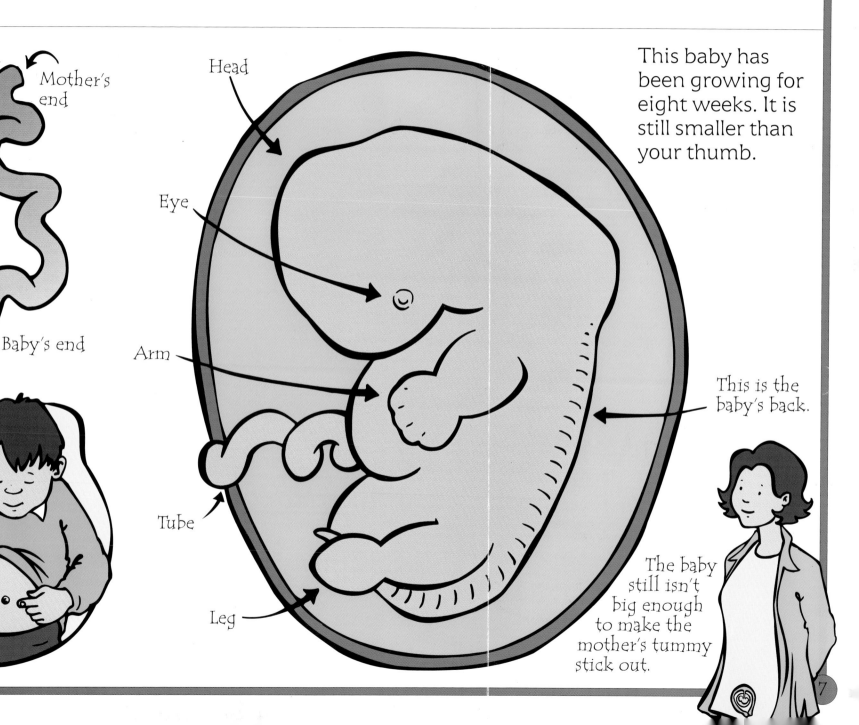

Mother's end

Baby's end

Head

Eye

Arm

Tube

Leg

This baby has been growing for eight weeks. It is still smaller than your thumb.

This is the baby's back.

The baby still isn't big enough to make the mother's tummy stick out.

# Look how quickly the baby grows!

This is the baby after just six weeks.

This will be the head.

This will be an eye.

This is the tube that carries food and drink from the mother.

This is the baby's real size.

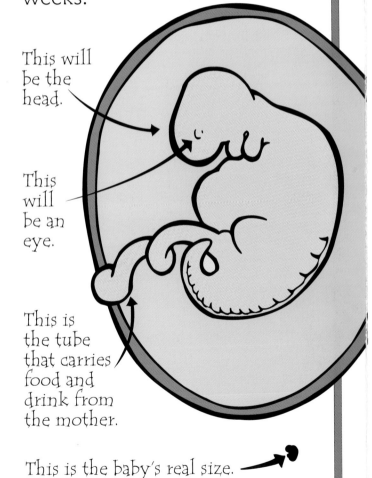

# Baby's getting big

The baby grows and grows inside the mother's womb. The womb is like a tough sack full of watery liquid.

## Starting to show

After about four months, the baby starts to make a bump in its mother's tummy.

Some of the time, the baby is awake. But most of the time it sleeps.

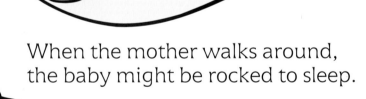

When the mother walks around, the baby might be rocked to sleep.

When the mother is still, the baby might wake up. It starts to move around.

# What does the baby do?

It does some of the things that you do.

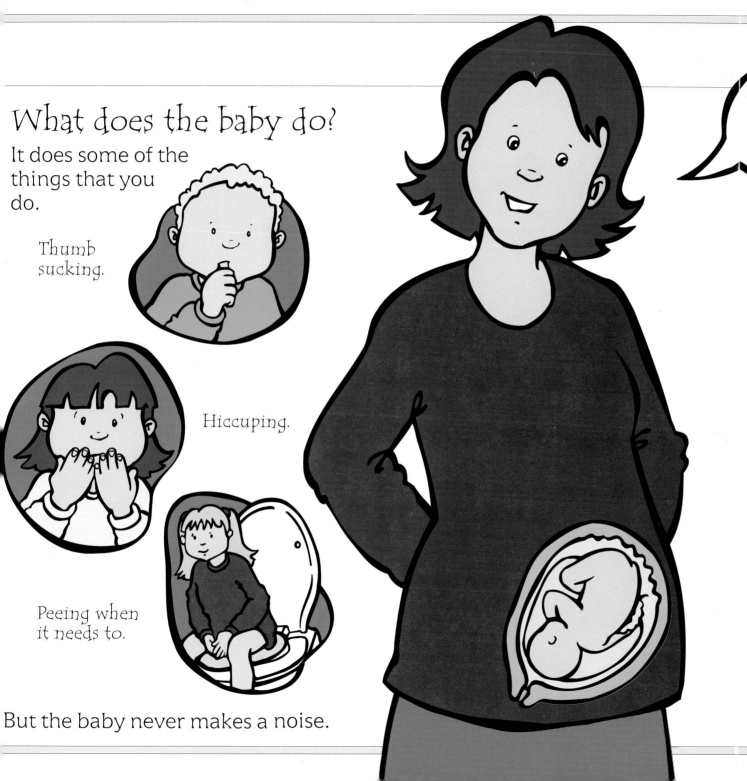

Thumb sucking.

Hiccuping.

Peeing when it needs to.

But the baby never makes a noise.

My baby has been inside for about six months.

## Safe from knocks

The liquid in the womb keeps the baby safe. Imagine carrying a fish in a plastic bag.

Even if you bump the bag, the fish doesn't get hurt. It's like that for the baby in the womb.

## Feeling the baby

Sometimes the mother can feel the baby move. It wiggles around inside her. It even rolls over and over.

Want to see the baby grow some more?

I've been growing for four months.

# Even bigger

The baby keeps getting bigger and bigger. It is heavy for the mother to carry inside her.

## Seeing

The baby's eyes work now. When it's awake, it opens its eyes. It can see colors and light coming in through its mother's skin.

This baby might see a warm red glow from the sun.

## Hearing

The baby's ears work. It hears things that happen inside its mother.

The baby can hear its mother's heart beating.

b-boom b-boom

gurgle gurgle

The baby can hear noises from its mother's stomach too.

chatter chatter

The baby can also hear things from outside.

# Lungs for breathing

When the baby is born, it will have to breathe air, like you do. You use your lungs to breathe.

This is where your lungs are.

The baby on the flap has been inside for about seven months.

# Will the baby get any bigger?

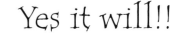

Whew! It's like carrying a big bag of groceries all the time.

# Yes it will!!

This baby is ready to be born. It has been inside for nine months. It takes up a lot of room inside the mother.

The baby makes the mother feel full and uncomfortable. She is ready for the baby to come out.

# Head down

The baby has moved around. It lies with its head facing down. When it is born, its head will come out first.

# The baby is ready

It is time for the baby to come out. The mother's womb starts to squeeze. It is pushing the baby out.

## Helping the mother

A nurse and a doctor look after the mother while she has her baby.

## Hard work

Getting the baby out can take hours. It makes the mother tired.

The baby squeezes out of the opening between the mother's legs.

Nurse

What happens next?

The baby is born!!

## What is it like for the baby?

Getting out is a tight squeeze for the baby.

The baby comes out from a place that is warm and cozy. Outside, it is brighter. Things are more lively and noisy.

The baby finds things strange.

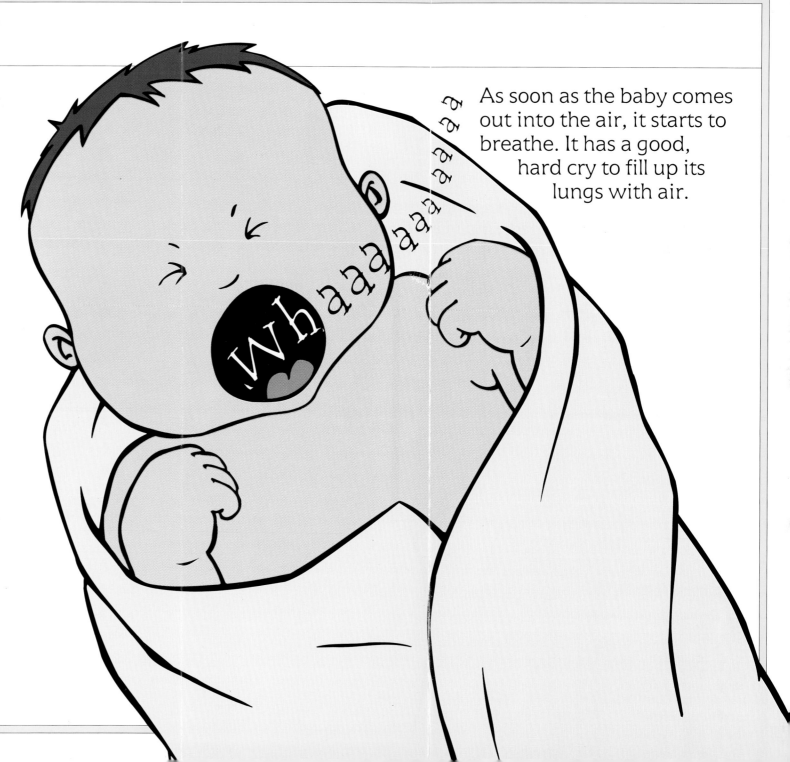

As soon as the baby comes out into the air, it starts to breathe. It has a good, hard cry to fill up its lungs with air.

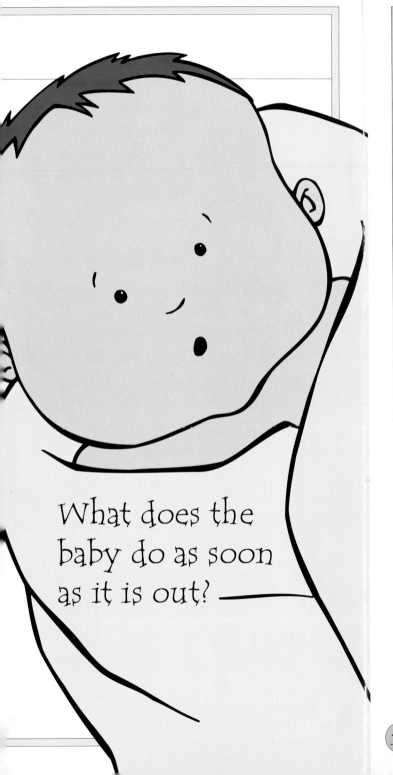

What does the baby do as soon as it is out?

# The new baby

The baby has been born. Now it does lots of new things. But first of all it is cuddled by its mother.

## What the baby does

The baby has milk for its food. The milk comes from its mother's breasts.

Mothers only make milk when they have a baby.

The baby has to wear diapers to stop its pee and poop from making a mess.

## Naming the baby

The mother and father choose a name for the baby.

Chris?... Jan?... Jamie?... Ali?... Frankie?...

Robin?... Jo?... Stevie?... Jamie?...

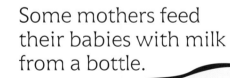

Some mothers feed their babies with milk from a bottle.

## Other things to do

The baby looks around. It can only see things very close to it. Things far away look fuzzy.

The baby pushes its arms and legs in and out. It wiggles its body around.

It sleeps!

The baby sleeps nearly all the time. It only wakes up when it wants some food.

The baby in this picture is about the same size as a real newborn baby.

Put your hand next to the baby's. See how much your hand has grown since you were born.

## That's the end of the story...

But it's only the beginning of the new baby's life.

## What does the baby do most?

# Index

Special thanks to Dr Sarah Bower, Consultant in Fetal Medicine and Obstetrics at Harris Birthright Trust, London, for advice in the writing of this book.

First published in 1997 by Usborne Publishing Ltd, 83-85 Saffron Hill, London EC1N 8RT, England.